CHECKERBOARD BIOGRAPHY LIBRARY

U.S. PRESIDENTS

The
United States Presidents

JOHN QUINCY ADAMS

John Quincy Adams

ABDO Publishing Company

Heidi M.D. Elston

visit us at
www.abdopublishing.com

Published by ABDO Publishing Company, 8000 West 78th Street, Edina, Minnesota 55439.
Copyright © 2009 by Abdo Consulting Group, Inc. International copyrights reserved in all
countries. No part of this book may be reproduced in any form without written permission from the
publisher. The Checkerboard Library™ is a trademark and logo of ABDO Publishing Company.

Printed in the United States.

Cover Photo: Getty Images
Interior Photos: Alamy pp. 10, 20, 27; Corbis pp. 5, 24; Getty Images pp. 19, 23, 28;
    iStockphoto p. 32; Library of Congress pp. 25, 29; Courtesy of the Massachusetts Historical
    Society p. 26; National Archives pp. 16, 18; National Park Service p. 9; North Wind pp. 8, 16,
    17, 21; Picture History pp. 11, 12, 13, 15

Editor: BreAnn Rumsch
Art Direction & Cover Design: Neil Klinepier
Interior Design: Jaime Martens

Library of Congress Cataloging-in-Publication Data

Elston, Heidi M.D., 1979-
 John Quincy Adams / Heidi M.D. Elston.
   p. cm. -- (The United States presidents)
 Includes index.
 ISBN 978-1-60453-440-5
 1. Adams, John Quincy, 1767-1848--Juvenile literature. 2. Presidents--United States--Biography--
Juvenile literature. I. Title.

 E377.E47 2009
 973.5'5092--dc22
 [B]

                         2008027048

CONTENTS

John Quincy Adams

John Quincy Adams was the sixth president of the United States. His father, John Adams, was the second U.S. president. This was the first time a son of a former U.S. president had become president.

Adams grew up during the **American Revolution**. As a child, he saw many battles near his home. He also traveled to Europe with his father. There, he gained much international experience.

As a young man, Adams was a lawyer and a writer. These experiences helped him start his political career as a successful diplomat. Later, Adams was elected to the U.S. Senate. He also worked as **secretary of state**.

Adams served one term as president. President Adams fought for what he believed was right. Along the way, he made many political enemies. They kept Adams from making improvements to the country he felt were necessary.

Following his time as president, Adams served 17 years in the U.S. House of Representatives. There, he fought the spread of slavery in the United States.

Throughout his adult life, Adams served his country at home and abroad. His work helped change the nation for the better. Today, Adams is remembered as one of America's greatest diplomats.

John Quincy Adams

TIMELINE

1767 - On July 11, John Quincy Adams was born in Braintree, Massachusetts.

1775 - Adams watched the battle of Bunker Hill, the first major battle of the American Revolution.

1778 - Adams joined his father in Europe.

1794 - Adams traveled to Europe as minister to the Netherlands.

1797 - On July 26, Adams married Louisa Catherine Johnson; Adams became minister to Prussia.

1802 - Adams won election to the Massachusetts state senate.

1803 - Adams was elected to the U.S. Senate.

1809 - President James Madison made Adams minister to Russia.

1814 - Adams worked to get the Treaty of Ghent signed. This ended the War of 1812.

1815 - Adams began serving as minister to Great Britain.

1817 - President James Monroe appointed Adams secretary of state.

1823 - Adams helped write the Monroe Doctrine.

1825 - On March 4, Adams became the sixth U.S. president.

1828 - Adams placed a tariff on imported industrial goods.

1830 - Adams was elected to the U.S. House of Representatives.

1841 - Adams defended the *Amistad* captives.

1848 - On February 23, John Quincy Adams died.

John Quincy Adams was the first president sworn in while wearing long pants. The first five presidents wore knickers, which are short, loose-fitting pants gathered at the knee.

On warm mornings, President Adams swam in the Potomac River. One day, reporter Anne Royall surprised him there. She sat on his clothes and refused to move until he gave her an interview. Before this, no female had interviewed a president.

Adams lived long enough to see the camera invented. Toward the end of his life, he had his picture taken. He is the first president of whom a photograph exists. Only three photographs are known to exist of Adams.

Louisa Adams was born in London, England, in 1775. She is the only first lady born outside of the United States.

WITNESSING HISTORY

John Quincy Adams was born on July 11, 1767, in Braintree, Massachusetts. The town was later renamed Quincy. John Quincy was the oldest son of John and Abigail Adams. He had an older sister and two younger brothers.

Abigail Adams

Young John Quincy saw U.S. history being made. He and his mother watched the battle of Bunker Hill near the family farm in 1775. It was the first major battle of the **American Revolution**. During the war, John Quincy's parents provided most of his education. John told young John Quincy about events that had led to the start of the American Revolution.

John Adams

FAST FACTS

BORN - July 11, 1767

WIFE - Louisa Catherine Johnson (1775–1852)

CHILDREN - 4

POLITICAL PARTY - Democratic-Republican

AGE AT INAUGURATION - 57

YEARS SERVED - 1825–1829

VICE PRESIDENT - John C. Calhoun

DIED - February 23, 1848, age 80

The oldest presidential birthplaces in the United States are in Quincy, Massachusetts. They are the John Quincy Adams birthplace (left) and the John Adams birthplace (right).

Young John Quincy

This included the Boston Massacre in 1770. During a **riot** in Boston, Massachusetts, British soldiers shot and killed five colonists. John had defended the soldiers in court.

John also told John Quincy about the Boston Tea Party. Colonists protested a tea tax in 1773. They dumped 342 chests of British tea into Boston Harbor.

In 1778, John went to Europe as a diplomat. John Quincy joined him. He lived throughout Europe for most of his teenage years.

From 1778 to 1779, John Quincy studied at a private school in Paris, France. There, he became **fluent** in French. John Quincy spent the next year at the University of Leiden in the Netherlands. During his brief stay, he became fluent in Dutch.

When he was 14, John Quincy went to Russia with Francis Dana. Dana was U.S. minister to Russia. John Quincy worked as his assistant. One year later, John Quincy joined his father in Paris. He helped John with the treaty that ended the **American Revolution**. This is called the Treaty of Paris.

In 1785, John Quincy returned to America. He had been well taught in history, mathematics, and classical languages such as Latin and Greek. John Quincy entered Harvard College in Cambridge, Massachusetts. He graduated in just two years.

After college, John Quincy decided to study law. In 1790, he became a lawyer. John Quincy then struggled to set up a law practice. Meanwhile, he began writing political newspaper articles. His articles caught President George Washington's attention. President Washington liked John Quincy's writings and made him minister to the Netherlands.

Francis Dana

DIPLOMAT

In 1794, Adams sailed to Europe to begin his diplomatic career. As minister, he reported to President Washington on events in the Netherlands and other European countries.

On a trip to London, England, Adams met Louisa Catherine Johnson. She was charming, warm, and well educated. Adams and Louisa were married on July 26, 1797.

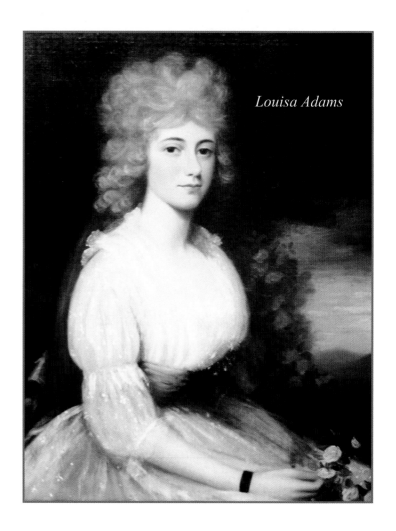

Louisa Adams

George Washington Adams

That year, Adams became minister to Prussia. So, he and Mrs. Adams moved to Prussia's capital, Berlin. Adams helped write a treaty with Prussia. He also traveled with his wife through Europe.

Mr. and Mrs. Adams's first child, George Washington Adams, was born in Berlin in 1801. He was named after President Washington. Later that year, the Adams family returned to Boston. There, Adams briefly worked as a lawyer.

SENATOR ADAMS

Soon, Adams decided to work in politics. In 1802, he was elected to the Massachusetts state senate. The next year, Adams won election to the U.S. Senate.

In 1807, President Thomas Jefferson called for a shipping **embargo**. Senator Adams supported the president. This action made him unpopular in New England. People there depended on shipping to make money. The next year, Adams quit the Senate.

Meanwhile, Mr. and Mrs. Adams had two more sons. John was born in 1803, and Charles Francis followed in 1807. A daughter named Louisa Catherine was born in 1811. Sadly, she died the next year.

In 1809, President James Madison made Adams minister to Russia. There, Adams saw French emperor Napoléon Bonaparte invade the country. As minister, Adams stayed in Europe to work for peace.

Adams's younger sons, John (left)
and Charles Francis (below)

SECRETARY ADAMS

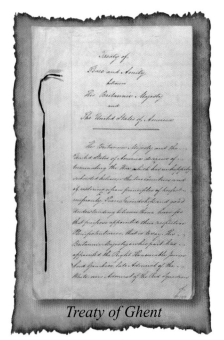

Treaty of Ghent

America and Great Britain fought each other in the **War of 1812**. In August 1814, Adams and a group of Americans went to Ghent, Belgium. They wanted to make peace with the British. Four months later, the Treaty of Ghent was signed.

Beginning in 1815, Adams served as minister to Great Britain. He and his family lived in a country house near London.

Adams returned to the United States in 1817. President James Monroe made him **secretary of state**.

At that time, Spain owned the Florida Territory. Adams made a deal with Spanish leaders. Spain agreed to give Florida to the United States. This was a great victory for the United States and for Adams.

President James Monroe

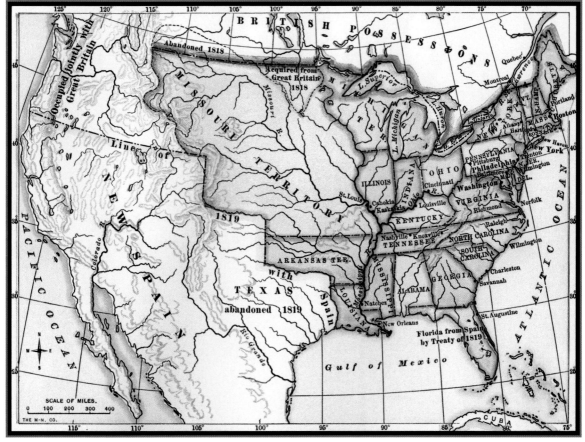

The United States in 1819

Secretary Adams's diplomatic success continued. In 1823, he helped write the Monroe Doctrine. It said that the United States supported North and South American colonies against European interference. Also, the United States would not allow Europeans to create new colonies in the Americas.

THE SIXTH PRESIDENT

Adams did well as **secretary of state**. Many historians consider Adams the finest secretary of state in American history.

In 1824, Adams decided to run for president as a

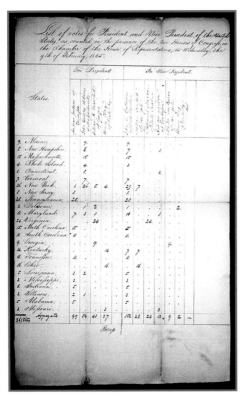

A record of the 1824 Electoral College votes

Democratic-Republican. Adams was one of five candidates. His opponents were **Secretary of the Treasury** William H. Crawford and **Speaker of the House** Henry Clay. Adams was also up against General Andrew Jackson and **Secretary of War** John C. Calhoun. Calhoun eventually withdrew from the contest and ran for vice president.

Jackson received 99 Electoral College votes. Adams won 84 votes, Crawford received 41, and Clay won 37. To win, a candidate needed more than half the total votes. None of the men had enough.

Going into the election, Adams had the support of the New England states.

According to the U.S. **Constitution**, the House of Representatives now had to choose the president. The House chose from the top three candidates. That meant Clay was out of the race.

Clay decided to back Adams. With Clay's support, Adams was elected the sixth U.S. president in February 1825. Calhoun won the vice presidency. On March 4, Adams was sworn into office.

President Adams wanted the best advisers for his **cabinet**. He refused to choose people based on the political party they belonged to.

Adams chose Clay as his **secretary of state**. Jackson's supporters in Congress protested. They claimed that Clay had helped Adams get elected so they could both get into office. Now, President Adams had political enemies in Congress.

Vice President Calhoun

PRESIDENT ADAMS'S CABINET

MARCH 4, 1825–
MARCH 4, 1829

STATE – Henry Clay
TREASURY – Richard Rush
WAR – James Barbour
      Peter B. Porter (from June 21, 1828)
NAVY – Samuel Lewis Southard
ATTORNEY GENERAL – William Wirt

Secretary of State Clay

RUNNING THE COUNTRY

President Adams wanted to advance America. In his **inaugural** address, he laid out a plan for many improvements. He wanted to build new roads and canals. He proposed establishing a national university and **observatory**. And, he wanted new laws to protect Native Americans.

But, President Adams still had many political enemies. Congress rejected most of his ideas. However, he did succeed in extending the Cumberland Road into Ohio. This road eventually stretched from Cumberland, Maryland, to Vandalia, Illinois. It opened up the West to settlement.

In 1828, President Adams signed a bill placing a **tariff** on imported industrial goods. Adams believed the tax would protect New England factories from foreign competition. Northerners supported the tariff, but Southerners opposed it. The tariff would

SUPREME COURT APPOINTMENT

ROBERT TRIMBLE - 1826

become a key issue in the 1828 election.

Throughout his presidency, Adams maintained a daily exercise routine. In the mornings, he swam in the Potomac River. He took long walks in the evenings. Adams also wrote daily in his diary and spent much time reading the Bible.

Although President Adams kept busy, he was sad about his battles with Congress. Adams held little hope for reelection in 1828.

Throughout his presidency, Adams's quarrels with Jackson continued.

THE ELECTION OF 1828

In 1828, President Adams entered one of the ugliest elections in U.S. history. He ran as a **National Republican**. **Secretary of the Treasury** Richard Rush was his **running mate**.

Andrew Jackson ran as a **Democrat**. Vice President Calhoun was Jackson's running mate.

The campaign was hateful. Both sides launched political and personal attacks against each other. The attacks harmed Adams's campaign. Jackson successfully won over most of the country. Adams had too many political enemies to win the election. Jackson received 178 electoral votes, and Adams won 83.

Adams took his defeat hard. He refused to attend Jackson's **inauguration**. In 1829, Adams returned to Quincy, Massachusetts.

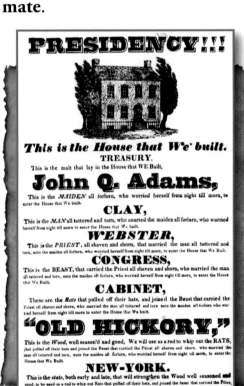

An election poster for Jackson

Andrew Jackson

OLD MAN ELOQUENT

Following his time as president, Adams planned to retire. But in 1830, he was elected to the U.S. House of Representatives. He served in the House for the rest of his life.

Adams had not been a popular president. But he was well liked and respected as a representative. Many congressmen admired the feeling he showed in his speeches. They called Adams "Old Man Eloquent."

Adams wrote in his diary about his election to the U.S. House of Representatives.

In Congress, Adams fought slavery. Congressmen from the South passed a series of gag rules. These rules banned any talk of slavery in the House. The gag rules kept laws against slavery from being passed. Adams fought the gag rules for eight years. Congress finally ended them in 1844.

Even when he faced bitter opposition, Adams fought for what he believed was right.

Throughout his life, Adams kept detailed diaries. These diaries provide much information about this former president.

In 1841, Representative Adams worked on an important law case. Two years earlier, a group of captive Africans had been on the slave ship *Amistad*. The Africans took control of the ship near Cuba. They sailed to the United States, where they were arrested. Adams became their lawyer. He fought for their freedom and won the case. They returned to Africa.

On February 21, 1848, Adams suffered a **stroke** on the floor of the House. Two days later, John Quincy Adams died in the U.S. Capitol. He is buried at United First Parish Church in Quincy.

Adams served his country and earned the nation's respect. He believed all Americans deserved to be free. So, he publicly opposed slavery. Adams is remembered as one of America's greatest diplomats. His patriotism helped him make peace with other countries. These contributions helped strengthen the country John Quincy Adams loved.

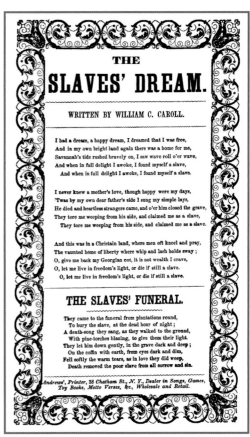

A slave song in which the writer dreams of freedom

OFFICE OF THE PRESIDENT

BRANCHES OF GOVERNMENT

The U.S. government is divided into three branches. They are the executive, legislative, and judicial branches. This division is called a separation of powers. Each branch has some power over the others. This is called a system of checks and balances.

EXECUTIVE BRANCH

The executive branch enforces laws. It is made up of the president, the vice president, and the president's cabinet. The president represents the United States around the world. He or she oversees relations with other countries and signs treaties. The president signs bills into law and appoints officials and federal judges. He or she also leads the military and manages government workers.

LEGISLATIVE BRANCH

The legislative branch makes laws, maintains the military, and regulates trade. It also has the power to declare war. This branch consists of the Senate and the House of Representatives. Together, these two houses make up Congress. Each state has two senators. A state's population determines the number of representatives it has.

JUDICIAL BRANCH

The judicial branch interprets laws. It consists of district courts, courts of appeals, and the Supreme Court. District courts try cases. If a person disagrees with a trial's outcome, he or she may appeal. If the courts of appeals support the ruling, a person may appeal to the Supreme Court. The Supreme Court also makes sure that laws follow the U.S. Constitution.

Qualifications for Office

To be president, a person must meet three requirements. A candidate must be at least 35 years old and a natural-born U.S. citizen. He or she must also have lived in the United States for at least 14 years.

Electoral College

The U.S. presidential election is an indirect election. Voters from each state choose electors to represent them in the Electoral College. The number of electors from each state is based on population. Each elector has one electoral vote. Electors are pledged to cast their vote for the candidate who receives the highest number of popular votes in their state. A candidate must receive the majority of Electoral College votes to win.

Term of Office

Each president may be elected to two four-year terms. Sometimes, a president may only be elected once. This happens if he or she served more than two years of the previous president's term.

The presidential election is held on the Tuesday after the first Monday in November. The president is sworn in on January 20 of the following year. At that time, he or she takes the oath of office:

I do solemnly swear (or affirm) that I will faithfully execute the office of President of the United States, and will to the best of my ability, preserve, protect and defend the Constitution of the United States.

LINE OF SUCCESSION

The Presidential Succession Act of 1947 defines who becomes president if the president cannot serve. The vice president is first in the line of succession. Next are the Speaker of the House and the President Pro Tempore of the Senate. If none of these individuals is able to serve, the office falls to the president's cabinet members. They would take office in the order in which each department was created:

Secretary of State

Secretary of the Treasury

Secretary of Defense

Attorney General

Secretary of the Interior

Secretary of Agriculture

Secretary of Commerce

Secretary of Labor

Secretary of Health and Human Services

Secretary of Housing and Urban Development

Secretary of Transportation

Secretary of Energy

Secretary of Education

Secretary of Veterans Affairs

Secretary of Homeland Security

BENEFITS

- While in office, the president receives a salary of $400,000 each year. He or she lives in the White House and has 24-hour Secret Service protection.

- The president may travel on a Boeing 747 jet called Air Force One. The airplane can accommodate 70 passengers. It has kitchens, a dining room, sleeping areas, and a conference room. It also has fully equipped offices with the latest communications systems. Air Force One can fly halfway around the world before needing to refuel. It can even refuel in flight!

- If the president wishes to travel by car, he or she uses Cadillac One. Cadillac One is a Cadillac Deville. It has been modified with heavy armor and communications systems. The president takes Cadillac One along when visiting other countries if secure transportation will be needed.

- The president also travels on a helicopter called Marine One. Like the presidential car, Marine One accompanies the president when traveling abroad if necessary.

- Sometimes, the president needs to get away and relax with family and friends. Camp David is the official presidential retreat. It is located in the cool, wooded mountains in Maryland. The U.S. Navy maintains the retreat, and the U.S. Marine Corps keeps it secure. The camp offers swimming, tennis, golf, and hiking.

- When the president leaves office, he or she receives Secret Service protection for ten more years. He or she also receives a yearly pension of $191,300 and funding for office space, supplies, and staff.

PRESIDENTS AND THEIR TERMS

PRESIDENT	PARTY	TOOK OFFICE	LEFT OFFICE	TERMS SERVED	VICE PRESIDENT
George Washington	None	April 30, 1789	March 4, 1797	Two	John Adams
John Adams	Federalist	March 4, 1797	March 4, 1801	One	Thomas Jefferson
Thomas Jefferson	Democratic-Republican	March 4, 1801	March 4, 1809	Two	Aaron Burr, George Clinton
James Madison	Democratic-Republican	March 4, 1809	March 4, 1817	Two	George Clinton, Elbridge Gerry
James Monroe	Democratic-Republican	March 4, 1817	March 4, 1825	Two	Daniel D. Tompkins
John Quincy Adams	Democratic-Republican	March 4, 1825	March 4, 1829	One	John C. Calhoun
Andrew Jackson	Democrat	March 4, 1829	March 4, 1837	Two	John C. Calhoun, Martin Van Buren
Martin Van Buren	Democrat	March 4, 1837	March 4, 1841	One	Richard M. Johnson
William H. Harrison	Whig	March 4, 1841	April 4, 1841	Died During First Term	John Tyler
John Tyler	Whig	April 6, 1841	March 4, 1845	Completed Harrison's Term	Office Vacant
James K. Polk	Democrat	March 4, 1845	March 4, 1849	One	George M. Dallas
Zachary Taylor	Whig	March 5, 1849	July 9, 1850	Died During First Term	Millard Fillmore

PRESIDENT	PARTY	TOOK OFFICE	LEFT OFFICE	TERMS SERVED	VICE PRESIDENT
Millard Fillmore	Whig	July 10, 1850	March 4, 1853	Completed Taylor's Term	Office Vacant
Franklin Pierce	Democrat	March 4, 1853	March 4, 1857	One	William R.D. King
James Buchanan	Democrat	March 4, 1857	March 4, 1861	One	John C. Breckinridge
Abraham Lincoln	Republican	March 4, 1861	April 15, 1865	Served One Term, Died During Second Term	Hannibal Hamlin, Andrew Johnson
Andrew Johnson	Democrat	April 15, 1865	March 4, 1869	Completed Lincoln's Second Term	Office Vacant
Ulysses S. Grant	Republican	March 4, 1869	March 4, 1877	Two	Schuyler Colfax, Henry Wilson
Rutherford B. Hayes	Republican	March 3, 1877	March 4, 1881	One	William A. Wheeler
James A. Garfield	Republican	March 4, 1881	September 19, 1881	Died During First Term	Chester Arthur
Chester Arthur	Republican	September 20, 1881	March 4, 1885	Completed Garfield's Term	Office Vacant
Grover Cleveland	Democrat	March 4, 1885	March 4, 1889	One	Thomas A. Hendricks
Benjamin Harrison	Republican	March 4, 1889	March 4, 1893	One	Levi P. Morton
Grover Cleveland	Democrat	March 4, 1893	March 4, 1897	One	Adlai E. Stevenson
William McKinley	Republican	March 4, 1897	September 14, 1901	Served One Term, Died During Second Term	Garret A. Hobart, Theodore Roosevelt

PRESIDENT	PARTY	TOOK OFFICE	LEFT OFFICE	TERMS SERVED	VICE PRESIDENT
Theodore Roosevelt	Republican	September 14, 1901	March 4, 1909	Completed McKinley's Second Term, Served One Term	Office Vacant, Charles Fairbanks
William Taft	Republican	March 4, 1909	March 4, 1913	One	James S. Sherman
Woodrow Wilson	Democrat	March 4, 1913	March 4, 1921	Two	Thomas R. Marshall
Warren G. Harding	Republican	March 4, 1921	August 2, 1923	Died During First Term	Calvin Coolidge
Calvin Coolidge	Republican	August 3, 1923	March 4, 1929	Completed Harding's Term, Served One Term	Office Vacant, Charles Dawes
Herbert Hoover	Republican	March 4, 1929	March 4, 1933	One	Charles Curtis
Franklin D. Roosevelt	Democrat	March 4, 1933	April 12, 1945	Served Three Terms, Died During Fourth Term	John Nance Garner, Henry A. Wallace, Harry S. Truman
Harry S. Truman	Democrat	April 12, 1945	January 20, 1953	Completed Roosevelt's Fourth Term, Served One Term	Office Vacant, Alben Barkley
Dwight D. Eisenhower	Republican	January 20, 1953	January 20, 1961	Two	Richard Nixon
John F. Kennedy	Democrat	January 20, 1961	November 22, 1963	Died During First Term	Lyndon B. Johnson
Lyndon B. Johnson	Democrat	November 22, 1963	January 20, 1969	Completed Kennedy's Term, Served One Term	Office Vacant, Hubert H. Humphrey
Richard Nixon	Republican	January 20, 1969	August 9, 1974	Completed First Term, Resigned During Second Term	Spiro T. Agnew, Gerald Ford

PRESIDENT	PARTY	TOOK OFFICE	LEFT OFFICE	TERMS SERVED	VICE PRESIDENT
Gerald Ford	Republican	August 9, 1974	January 20, 1977	Completed Nixon's Second Term	Nelson A. Rockefeller
Jimmy Carter	Democrat	January 20, 1977	January 20, 1981	One	Walter Mondale
Ronald Reagan	Republican	January 20, 1981	January 20, 1989	Two	George H.W. Bush
George H.W. Bush	Republican	January 20, 1989	January 20, 1993	One	Dan Quayle
Bill Clinton	Democrat	January 20, 1993	January 20, 2001	Two	Al Gore
George W. Bush	Republican	January 20, 2001	January 20, 2009	Two	Dick Cheney
Barack Obama	Democrat	January 20, 2009			Joe Biden

"If your actions inspire others to dream more, learn more, do more and become more, you are a leader." John Quincy Adams

WRITE TO THE PRESIDENT

You may write to the president at:

The White House
1600 Pennsylvania Avenue NW
Washington, DC 20500

You may e-mail the president at:
comments@whitehouse.gov

GLOSSARY

American Revolution - from 1775 to 1783. A war for independence between Great Britain and its North American colonies. The colonists won and created the United States of America.

cabinet - a group of advisers chosen by the president to lead government departments.

Constitution - the laws that govern the United States.

Democrat - a member of the Democratic political party. When John Quincy Adams was president, Democrats supported farmers and landowners.

Democratic-Republican - a member of the Democratic-Republican political party. During the early 1800s, Democratic-Republicans believed in weak national government and strong state government.

embargo - an order of a government banning the departure of commercial ships from its ports.

fluent - able to speak clearly and easily in a particular language.

inauguration (ih-naw-gyuh-RAY-shuhn) - a ceremony in which a person is sworn into office.

National Republican - a member of the National Republican political party. National Republicans opposed Andrew Jackson and believed in Henry Clay's program of high tariffs, internal improvements, and a national bank.

observatory - an institution whose primary purpose is making observations of happenings of nature.

riot - a sometimes violent disturbance caused by a large group of people.

running mate - a candidate running for a lower-rank position on an election ticket, especially the candidate for vice president.

secretary of state - a member of the president's cabinet who handles relations with other countries.

secretary of the treasury - a member of the president's cabinet that heads the U.S. Department of the Treasury. The secretary advises the president on financial policies and reports to Congress on the nation's finances. The secretary of the treasury is the U.S. government's chief financial officer.

secretary of war - a member of the president's cabinet who handles the nation's defense.

Speaker of the House - the highest-ranking member of the party with the majority in Congress.

stroke - a sudden loss of consciousness, sensation, and voluntary motion. This attack of paralysis is caused by a rupture to a blood vessel of the brain, often caused by a blood clot.

tariff - the taxes a government puts on imported or exported goods.

War of 1812 - from 1812 to 1814. A war fought between the United States and Great Britain over shipping rights and the capture of U.S. soldiers.

WEB SITES

To learn more about John Quincy Adams, visit ABDO Publishing Company on the World Wide Web at **www.abdopublishing.com**. Web sites about John Quincy Adams are featured on our Book Links page. These links are routinely monitored and updated to provide the most current information available.

INDEX